PHAETON AND THE SUN CHARIOT

ZEUS SHINING

DIONYSUS AND THE PIRATES

For Holly and Lara

ORCHARD BOOKS
96 Leonard Street, London EC2A 4XD
Orchard Books Australia
Unit 31/56 O'Riordan Street, Alexandria, NSW 2015
This text was first published in Great Britain in the form of
a gift collection called *The Orchard Book of Greek Gods and Goddesses*,
illustrated by Emma Chichester Clark in 1997
This edition first published in hardback in Great Britain in 2000
First paperback publication 2001
Text © Geraldine McCaughrean 1997
Illustrations © Tony Ross 2000
The rights of Geraldine McCaughrean to be identified as the author and
Tony Ross as the illustrator of this work have been asserted by them in
accordance with the Copyright, Designs, and Patents Act, 1988
ISBN 1 84121 895 2 (hardback)
ISBN 1 84121 656 9 (paperback)
1 3 5 7 9 10 8 6 4 2 (hardback)
1 3 5 7 9 10 8 6 4 2 (paperback)
A CIP catalogue record for this book is available
from the British Library
Printed in Great Britain

DUDLEY PUBLIC LIBRARIES

The loan of this book may be renewed if not required by other readers, by contacting the Library from which it was borrowed.

CP/494

Schools Library and Information Service

PHAETON AND THE SUN CHARIOT

ZEUS SHINING

DIONYSUS AND THE PIRATES

GERALDINE MCCAUGHREAN
ILLUSTRATED BY TONY ROSS

ORCHARD BOOKS

PHAETON AND THE SUN CHARIOT

Once, the weather was always pleasant, no matter where, no matter when. Each day, as now, the sun god Helios mounted his fiery chariot and rode through the Portals of Dawn, up into the sky. Nothing deflected him from his path across the blue cosmos, though each day the route changed a little, according to season.

It was from up there that he saw the nymph Clymene and fell in love with her. They had three girls and a boy – Phaeton – and although the girls were content to help their father harness the horses to his sun chariot, Phaeton wanted more.

"May I drive, Father? May I? One day? May I, please?"

"No," said Helios. "You haven't the strength. You haven't the art. The task is mine, and too much depends on it."

But Phaeton kept on wheedling and pleading for a chance to drive the chariot, and his foolish mother joined in on his behalf. "Let him, Helios. Let him drive it. Just once. Then perhaps he'll give us some peace."

"No," said Helios.

But Phaeton was a spoilt boy and accustomed to getting his way. At last he wore out the patience of Helios.

"Drive it, then! But for my sake and your own – take care. Drive no faster than I drive, and keep to the appointed path!"

Angry at himself for giving in, Helios withdrew to a turret of dark cloud, away from his pestering family.

Laughing and teasing, Phaeton's sisters happily harnessed the horses. Nostrils flared, hoofs stamping, the horses sensed an unfamiliar weight on the running board, unfamiliar hands on the reins. And no sooner did Phaeton lay hold of his father's golden whip than he cracked it in their ears.

From standing, they leapt to a gallop, eyes rolling, teeth clenching the bit between their teeth. Dawn that day was a flash of orange on the horizon, and then it was noon.

This was thrilling, exhilarating! Phaeton gave a whoop of triumph and braced his knees against the chariot sides. Perhaps a little slower, he thought. But when he did draw back on the reins, the stallions simply reared up and tossed their heads, wrenching his arms in their sockets, burning his hands as the reins pulled through his fingers. The chariot wheels left their well-trodden track.

To left and right the chariot slewed, evaporating cloudbanks, scorching flocks of birds. The world's soothsayers looked up and foretold miracles and catastrophes, as the sun zigzagged around the sky.

Phaeton tried to take control by flogging the horses with the golden whip. "Stop, I said! Slow down! Stop!" But the stallions only panicked under the whip, ducked their heads and ploughed downwards – down towards the Earth.

Where the fiery blaze of the chariot passed close to the

Earth, its forests caught fire, and black smoke rose off waving fields of flame. Rivers turned to steam, lakes boiled, and even the shallow fringes of the sea dried to saltpans, white and peppered with dying fish.

Phaeton pulled on the reins till his fingers bled. At the last moment, the horses lifted their heads before they could crash into the Earth. But now they stampeded so high into the sky that the air was too thin to breathe.

Far below, the Earth was robbed of its warmth; crops died, the sea froze. Sweat streaming from the necks of Helios' horses fell in large, fluffy flakes, and rivers slowed into glaciers of ice.

The blood vessels standing proud on their sweat-dark necks, the horses plunged up and down, to and fro in a frenzy of panic. And beneath them the face of the Earth was transformed for ever – burnt or frozen or flooded. The animals found their habitats transformed.

The bears went north,
seeking coolness,

the penguins went south.

Monkeys fled jabbering
to the jungles

and the people sought shade
or warmth.

Phaeton hauled on the reins till the reins frayed through on the chariot's copper

prow, and snapped.

Helios emerged from his turret of cloud, his face white as the moon. "What have you done?" he howled.

Zeus emerged from the Cloudy Citadel. "What have you done, Helios, letting a child play with your chariot? My world is in ruins, and what ruin is still to come if he isn't stopped?" From his armoury of thunderbolts, Zeus took the largest.

"No! No! Not my son!" screamed Clymene.

"No! No! Not Phaeton!" cried his sisters.

Zeus glared at Helios, and the sun god bowed his head. "It is the only way," he agreed.

The thunderbolt flew with perfect aim as Phaeton clung in terror to the wildly veering chariot. It struck him on the forehead and he fell without a cry, terribly slowly, somersaulting and wheeling through clouds, past skeins of geese, and into the blue of the sea. The broken reins were found still gripped in his hands when his sisters carried him ashore and buried him.

Three tall slender exclamations of grief, they stood by his grave swaying and moaning. "It was our fault," they wept. "We helped to harness the horses."

But it was no one's fault but Phaeton's. Too proud, too rash, too spoilt, and too stupid, he brought ruin to whole tracts of his planet, and shame to his father.

Seeing the three sisters, Zeus took pity on them and turned them into poplar trees, tall, slender and waving. But still they wept, tears of amber welling through their bark in big golden drops which caught the sun.

ZEUS SHINING

Listen! Is that thunder? Zeus and Hera must be quarrelling again. Once, when Hera was particularly spiteful to one of his mortal sons, Zeus hung her over a cliff with an anvil tied to her feet. But all that did was make her three spans taller and put her in a bad temper for a century. And she could always find a way of getting back at her husband.

Semele, Princess of Thebes, was so pretty that Zeus fell in love with her as easily as a pebble falls into a pond. Of course he visited her not in his own magnificent shape, but disguised as an ordinary mortal. She knew who he was, but was not silly enough to take advantage. For instance, she did not ask for magical presents, or to visit Olympus or to live for ever. Zeus loved her all the more for that.

Then Hera found out. Amazingly, she did not send monsters to imprison Semele, did not conjure sharks from the sea to devour her, did not hurl boulders at her out of Heaven's windows. No, she just went and spoke to her, as one woman to another.

"I quite understand," she said smiling ever so sweetly. "How could you – how could anyone resist the Almighty, the Shining Zeus. Though you've never actually *seen* Zeus in all his glory, have you? Oh, you poor little thing! Never to see the true nature of your lover! How unbearable!"

"I don't mind. Really," said Semele. But her curiosity had been aroused. What *did* he really look like, her marvellous immortal? She was expecting his baby by now: who would the baby look like? Her or the Shining Zeus?

The very next time Zeus visited her, she asked him, "Show me yourself in your true radiance, my love! Show me the Zeus I have never seen. Show me Zeus shining!"

"No!" said Zeus. "I couldn't possibly. You are a mortal woman with mortal eyes. No! Don't ask again."

But Semele could not put it out of her mind. It gnawed on her day and night – not knowing, not being allowed to know.

"You don't love me," she told Zeus. "You don't care one fig or grape for me, if you won't let me see you shining."

"No," said Zeus, and stopped her mouth with kisses.

"You love Hera more than you love me," said Semele the next time. "*She's* seen you, but I never have. Let me. Please? Please!"

"No!" said Zeus, and went home early, slamming the door.

"I think if I don't see you, I shall die," said Semele, stroking her big stomach and crying bitterly, "and then what will become of this baby of ours?"

Whether she won him round, or
whether he just lost his temper, Zeus
did show himself to Princess Semele.
He pulled on his cloak, turned round
three times, and passed his hands twice
over his face and hair.

A thousand shadows danced on the
walls of that little Theban palace, cast
by a bright profusion of lights. Then the
shadows themselves were burnt away – so
were the walls – and the garden beyond –
and the trees in the neighbouring orchard.

Recovering his true
shape, Zeus grew to
such a size that he
shattered the palace,
like a phoenix
hatching from its
egg. And like an
incandescent flame,
his glory scorched
everything for miles
around, set it ablaze.
Semele was frizzled
up like a moth in a
candle flame.

Tears were still wet
on Zeus's cheeks when
he summoned Hermes,
messenger of the gods, Hermes the helper.
He had something in his fist – something
small and fragile: an egg, Hermes thought.

"Can you find a safe place for this, boy?" he said. "It is all that is left to me of a great love." Unfolding his fingers one by one, he showed...Semele's unborn baby, only half formed, only halfway to being alive.

Quickly Hermes fetched a knife and cut open Zeus's thigh. Placing the unformed child inside the wound, he stitched it shut.

"You realise the child will be immortal now?" Hermes said. "Born of a god."

His tears dried. His face broke into a grin.

"Oh dear," said Shining Zeus. "*Won't* Queen Hera be vexed."

A few weeks later, Zeus had all but forgotten Semele. Being a god, the only pain he generally felt was a nagging headache. But today a sudden sharp cramp made him snatch at his thigh. Out from between the great sinews, out through the shining, scarred skin, Dionysus was born, god of growing things, god of the vines.

Zeus called for wine and raised a toast on Olympus's snowy peak. "To Dionysus, my immortal son!" he said.

And the rage in Hera's eyes burned as red as the embers still glowing far below among the ashes of Thebes.

DIONYSUS AND THE PIRATES

Life and soul of the party, that's how people
described him. Popular? Of course he was!
He was the god of wine, and wherever
Dionysus was, a free drink was never far
away. Like seagulls behind a fishing boat,
his drunken followers screeched and
swooped along behind him, singing,
dancing and falling over. In fact, he moved
amid a raucous, rambling party which never
ended until the last centaur, satyr, nymph
or votary had keeled over and fallen asleep.

But Dionysus was not a drunkard. He had no red nose, no rolling eyes or rubbery legs: he did not drink that much. Indeed, he was a fine-looking young man with the strong, fit body of an athlete. And for all he had been brought up by the fun-loving satyrs – they'd taught him all the songs and jokes he knew! – he also liked peace and solitude. So one day, when his hangers-on had all fallen off, as it were, and lay fast asleep in the grass, Dionysus went and stood on a jutting cliff, simply looking out to the sea. The wind billowed his purple cloak and ruffled his curling black hair.

A band of pirates saw him there, and
thought at once, "A slave! We can sell a
strapping boy like that in Africa, for
gold!" Creeping up, all slithering quiet,
with knives between their teeth, they
pounced on Dionysus and bundled him
aboard their pirate dhow.

The god was intrigued. Nothing like this
had ever happened to him before.

They tried to tie him to the mast. But whether they used clove hitches or reef knots, round turns or splices, the rope simply slipped down round the god's ankles like wet seaweed. At last, out of curiosity, he allowed them to tie him tight.

"Do you know who I am?" he asked.

"Don't know. Don't care," snarled the captain. "Will your father pay a ransom or your mother give her jewels to get you back? If not, we'll take you to Africa and sell you for a slave!"

"Oh, I wouldn't do that, if I were you," said Dionysus.

The pirates laughed hollowly. "Out here on the sea, our word is law. We do as we like and like what we do. And if you don't – well, Mr Slave, how do you plan to stop us?"

Dionysus did not answer, but took in
a deep, deep breath. He took in the north
wind, the south and the east. He took in
the west wind and a flying fish or two. The
sails drooped and the pirate ship slowed
to a standstill, rocking on the swell. The
pirates licked their fingers and held them
in the air. Not a breath of wind.

"We're becalmed, Captain!"

Now the pirates thought this strange, but
they did not think to blame their prisoner
for the sudden change in the weather. They
caught some fish and they counted some
loot and they drank some stolen wine.

"You like wine, do you?" said Dionysus.
All the pirates laughed and drank to
slavery – all except the steersman, who
brought Dionysus a cup of water. The sun
was very hot.

Emptying his flagon, the captain hurled it
overboard in disgust.

"More wine, Captain?" said Dionysus,
and whistled high and long.

The prow lifted and the ship yawed. A
tide race swelled the ripples into waves,
and plaited the waves
into mighty combers.
Then their colour
deepened, like a
bruise, to purple,
and bubbles rose
silvery to the
surface. So did
the fish, to sing.

Not until giant waves began to break over the ship did the pirates fully grasp that the sea had turned to wine. They licked the spray off their faces; they sucked their sodden shirts; they ran to and fro with hammocks to try and catch the wine that washed over the deck.

They lowered so many buckets that
the ship was towed along on the raging
current of wine.

"*He* did it! *He* did it!"
cried the steersman.
"Ask him who he is!"

"I am Dionysus, god
of wine," said the
prisoner. "Now take
me ashore if you please."

But the pirate captain did
nothing of the sort. "You? A god? Then
I'm the King of the Dryads. But a magician
I can sell to the circus for
more than the price of a
slave. So let's see some
more of your magic!"

From stem to
stern, the rigging
shone dark green,
and began to sprout. It
put on leaves, it put on
shoots and twining tendrils.

And climbing the ropes and mast and
rails, a whole vineyard of the ship.
Pale green grapes ripened into
black – so many and such
heavy grapes that the
ship sank lower
and lower into
the running sea.

First the sailors tried to fill the holds,
but when the holds were full, and still the
grapes kept growing, they slashed them
down in panic and threw them overboard.

The juice ran into their armpits, the
juice dripped into their eyes. It stuck
their beards to their chests and their feet
slid from under them. But they slashed
and slashed with cutlasses and knives, till
the vines turned back to rope again, and
the ship's rigging lay in little strands
and cords around their feet.

Dionysus shook off the ropes and ran his fingers through his hair.

"Enough, your honour!" begged the steersman. "We see now the power of the gods!"

"A cod for the gods!" roared the captain. "This magician is too good for the circus. I shall keep him and grow rich! Grapes and wine? What else can you do?"

At that, the god Dionysus rather lost patience with the pirates. "I am Dionysus, god of wine, god of growing things, Olympian son of Zeus, immortal as the sea! I have spoken soft and I have spoken plain. I have given you due warning. What can I do? *See what I can do!*"

The sky turned black. In outstretched hands, the god caught thunderbolts as they fell, and began to juggle them, along with crooked blades of lightning and members of the crew.

When he whistled this time, sea monsters rose from the deepest sea trenches, with goggling eyes and gaping mouths and mile-long tentacles.

He stamped, and stampeded the sea
god's horses. He blew, and in blowing,
borrowed the winds of Heaven. He
spun that ship like a spinning top,
and the moon came up wine-red.

Dionysus leapt to the crow's-nest,
where phosphorescent fire blazed in
a burning ball. And when he leapt
down again, Dionysus was a lion.

"Abandon ship! Abandon ship!" yelled
the captain, as the lion chased him from
tiller to taffrail, from prow to poop,
chewing his plaited hair.

"Swim for your lives!" yelled the pirates,
as one by one they plunged overboard,
into the heaving sea.

The sea subsided and the sky cleared.
The lion stretched out in the sunshine,
and a breeze began to blow. The steersman
was in the crow's-nest, but no one else was
aboard. Around the ship, leaping and
rolling, exchanging stuttering cries, a dozen
silvery creatures swam in a turquoise sea.

"I have never seen the like, your honour,"
said the steersman, watching their circus
tumbling. "What will you
name them?"

"I think I shall
call them 'dolphins',"
said Dionysus,
recovering his
usual shape. Then,
wrapping himself
in his purple cloak,
he walked home
across the sea.

So now dolphins cruise the world's green oceans, and patrol the navy seas. At the sight of a ship they leap for joy. At the sight of a sailor they dance on their tails. It is said that, in terrible shipwrecks, they have even rescued the crew, carried them home to shallow waters, with grins on their beaky mouths. Are they trying to earn forgiveness, for the time they insulted a god?